KNOWING LOVE

A Journey of Discovery

Other books by Elizabeth Jo

Choosing New Ways Forward

Book 1: Shifting Our Relationship with Trauma

Book 2: How Do I Get to be Me?

CHOOSING NEW WAYS FORWARD
BOOK 3

KNOWING LOVE

A Journey of Discovery

Elizabeth Jo

Henschel
HAUS
Milwaukee, Wisconsin

Cover art by Elizabeth Jo

Published by HenschelHAUS Publishing, Inc.
www.henschelHAUSbooks.com
Milwaukee, Wisconsin

ISBN: 978159598-979-6
LCCN: 2023948718

For love of sound

Welcome

to a journey of discovery

As we traverse

time and space,

Love's conversation

is weaving unfolding moments

that invite us to know her more fully

as we discover our own infinite presence

This epic journey is beginning

let's lean in and listen ...

Where time and space pulse in oceanic unison

a diver enters the night sky

folding into ink so deep

that shimmering starlight

swirls without shadow

and yet, on occasion like tonight, leaves a trail

an unanticipated thread

that ripples

As this arc drifts overhead

on an exhale of cool euphoria

Love inhales, riding currents

of creation

Opening her heart

to shape virgining threads,

she reaches forward

inviting new conversation

to the weaving

Love has come to the thawing river

that flows amongst still naked trees

as winter melts into spring

She builds a fire

and places rocks for sitting, in a circle

all around

Little Giants join her here

(ever close and always near)

perched on branch

so very tiny,

Giant Love

for all to hear.

On this boundless night,

Love is reflecting herself

as never before

Strands

in her weaving

have forgotten

they are treasured

and connected

pulsing threads of life

Swaddled in starlit cloth,

Little Giants lean in

Love whispers …

"We have new beginnings in our continuum

Opportunity has rippled the weaving

Fabric is unfolding to a crescendo

In pitch of night, a steady pulse is sounding

"Humans are wandering,

searching for a path

their path

They are seeking a place,

their place

In fabric that flows,

that moves with the weaving

Humans have forgotten

they know

the thread and the pulse

Love sounding,

echoing

within

"This is the opportunity,

a gift

To see anew

what is there

for the seeing

To live in the knowing

of what is

already known

– as though

for the very first time

"Once Upon a Time ..."

Flames spark, tears

gather, spilling

over Love's cheeks

Her lips form a grin

a melody caresses the weaving,

saturating the fabric, sating existence

Little Giants take each other's hands

holding gentleness, together

Upon this time

Where each thread belongs,

continuously forming

pattern that weaves

Threads of the weaving

are taking new form

Individual voices are

creating expressions

to join around the fire

Love has done this before

long ago, when human life

began

Yet, she is sure

these threads will always know

their part

and never feel apart

Curiosity and Creativity

rise with the weaving

to rest their threads in her hands

(Little Giants feel stirrings,

like goldfish swimming in their stomachs)

Once formed,

Curiosity and Creativity

jump to earth

growing into their height

before scampering through trees, in search

of wood for fire

These versatile weavings,

as all weavings are,

glow from within

illuminating their way

They traverse forest floor,

tall and reaching

only to become round and rollie

rollie-pollie seekers of chewy chunky wood

Mucky brown leaves

separate from snow melt

to greet familiar friends

buzzing to and fro

For, we know

each thread

recognizes each element

as gatherings grow

in this forested night

As weaving flows,

Curiosity and Creativity frequently

collaborate with Invention

when wondering delight

moves with intention

On this magical night

Invention tumbles past tall trees

pulling shiny red cart

on soft friendly breeze

Together, three friends

stack wood that's

eager to traverse

where conversation is gathering

Love hears jangling

beyond fire's reach

where singing squirrels jingle

and caws jamber

joyful jubilee

Standing now, Little Giants

clap their hands

as music dances and plays

'round red cart

resplendent with wood

Love sooths the weaving,

smoothing each thread

when a fourth rests in her palm

Cupping her fingers,

Possibility's feet

begin to form

knees growing round

Blink of an eye,

Possibility bounds 'round

tall hat tilting deepest-purple

greeting to contemplative spider

Nervously flapping

hawk lightly lands

where purple perch moves

to rest on thick curls

Love laughs

Possibility takes a bow

(nearly up-ending hawk)

and together with spider

three take a seat on the rock to the right

Drawn by joy's cascading scent,

Ease reaches out to tickle Love's skin

Ease grows as it goes

reaching through fire's middle

to sit on a rock

across the circle from Love

Legs crossed, Ease whistles

a whimsical tune

when Creativity bursts through trees

Curiosity follows pulling red cart

brimming with wood and Invention,

who sits on the tailgate

dangling toes in starlit night

Echoing stability

of a sundrenched afternoon

Presence moves with grace,

traversing Love's hand

tickling her fingertips

Presence pirouettes from Love's thumb

to index finger

before leaping left

with a "plop"

Abundance soon follows,

threading red, green, then blue

that burst into arms, pop into

legs, bloom into hair

Flowing to the right, Abundance

hugs each

before straddling

the rock next to Ease

Jumping up

Abundance adds a large log to fire,

grinning as swirling flames

dance revolutions

Little Giants applaud

Love shifts the weaving to her shoulders

Taking a breath,

she fills herself

to her toes

Curiosity wiggles

Few words

in a long train of questions

glide smoothly to Love's ear,

"What's this about?"

Presence stands,

bits of orange and sky blue

ride rain drops, "plop ka-plop plop ka-plop,"

around the circle

"plop pop ka-plop," spring's

caravan drenching

dappled air

Ease reaches deep

where bulging pocket

holds bits of blue lint and

Innocence, who wiggles

perky ears bouncing

Love's embrace

cradles the forest,

"It's lovely to be here

gathering in undividable

individuality

Yet, moving along weaving's path

humans are living divided, separate lives."

Presence leans in, "Separate?"

Innocence skittles around

to perch on Love's foot

Nose twitching, "What does this mean?"

Creativity snatches-up a doodlings stick,

clacks and clicks

forming wonderings

of a "separate" track.

Love reaches down, tickling

curious ears

Her voice follows the strand,

"There is a sound that sways with the river

and flows through life's fabric.

"Sound is recognized, heard

It is known as whisper,

as hurricane blows,

and, when taking breath,

does not snail's

antennae twitch."

Nods bob around crackling fire

Love continues,

"And, I've also heard noise."

Again, there's a pause.

Elbows meet knees, chins

rest on palms, brows join in wonder

"From what I have heard," Love continues,

"noise rises in a *Gap*

In fact, there's a saying, *Mind the Gap.*'"

Laughter quiets, Love adds,

"Ah, but it's true. There are those

who are of us

believing in this *Gap*."

Leaving space for breath,

she passes plump purple plums

Juice squirts in newly formed

mouths gone dry

Invention offers tart sweet fruit

to Little Giant hands

before returning to the fire

where Love swallows,

"I've heard what you guess – noise

rises from this space,

this crack where continuous

has been re-imagined

as burden and strife,

creating

Gap."

Creativity drops stick,

fluttering to Invention's side

Wondering feet shuffle,

noddings of

amazed exclamation

bobble furrowing brows

Eventually, Invention's voice rises,

"That is both clever and creative,

this we do see. And we clearly must wonder,

'How can this be?'

Each tree and each word,

every note

is arc – joined.

What of this *Gap*?

Fabric must flow

so that any can float!

What's

this then, that's creating?

How can moving be free??"

"Ah," Love begins,

"this then is the tangle I see!

Human threads have said,

'Connection's not real.'

Persons believe in

somewheres – sometimes

when Only noise, without sound,

is all … all that must be."

River gulps,

a gust plummets through,

frozen bits

reach water

and flow

"Oh!" Abundance exclaims, "We will not

tangle in noise! Nor know absence of sound!

Threads pulse Love

in all hearts. Together,

yes, together we stay In our Tune!"

Love reaches over to Presence

Hand in hand, the circle joins

Creativity starts with "mmmm"

that grows to "Hmmmm"

Curiosity joins in,

"What of the tangle,

where jingle collides

and jangle splinters

across the floor?"

Presence tones harmony, deep and strong,

"Where wings are caught

by hearts distraught?

Where hands aren't joined?

Where breath isn't breathed?"

Little Giants chime in chorus,

"What about, bum-ta-bum,

the tangle?"

All join the tune, "Bum-ta-da-Bum"

Music wafts across treetops

Love moves alongside fire

adding a branch, warming her hands,

"I have an idea."

Looking around the circle, she offers,

"As Love, as we who remember our loving,

we can speak together – 'individually,'

the way Persons have grown

in habit of hearing

We can speak our love,

our wonder and care

We can speak

our presence, abundance and ease

Possibility and invention will be

new and free

when curiosity and creativity

are Love known to be."

Hawk soars

carrying Little Giants in circles

that widen to include the entire forest

As spider begins new webs

of connection,

Possibility pulls canvas

from hat, resting it on easel

in fire's light

With Love's touch, white cloth

shows a room,

our circle expands

Peeking into canvas

no longer blank,

all thrill

when Person they see

Curiosity steps

forward to rest fingers

on sunrise

Person swings legs

over bed's edge

Have To steps onto carpet.

Curiosity blinks as from a dream

Catching a breath, turning to

friends gathered near,

"Where is wonder on this embarking of day?

What has *Have To*

to do with such brilliant display?

Sun welcomes possibility, yet

how will dear ones now truly meet?"

Ease moves to Curiosity's side

Person drops spoon past

coffee cup's edge.

Won't Get There

stirs a differing day.

Standing on shoulder of Ease,

Innocence tickles

curious spark into

the brew

The moment

lights Person's eyes before

Better slides in

Spoon full of sweetener

drawing a curtain,

sugarcoating the day.

As if on cue, Possibility offers

Person a daisy

setting it gently

on windowsill

in morning's light

Smile lifts Person's cheeks to warm glow,

fingers reach to embrace the moment

perhaps share it,

when *Less Than* sidles between

fingerprint and stem

alerting Person to *Alone*.

Smelling current on air,

Abundance, Creativity and Invention

join together, lifting windowpane

Smooth twinkle wafts in

carrying sparrow song

across Person's willowy frame

jiggling pajamas

with delightful shimmer

Coffee cup in lighter grip,

Person starts for bathroom

when

Stuck echoes with *Don't Want*,

tightening clench

along Person's jaw

as day looms in hall

between tap water and bathwater.

Presence touches swirling thought,

reaching to tap Person's heart

orient the day

Awe and surprise pass through our group

when Person turns

averting heart-opening Presence.

Each of those gathered

releases a gasp

Noses toward canvas pressed, turn

to hear what Love will say

"Persons are afraid," she whispers

into waves astonished

"Afraid?"

"Afraid of what?"

Possibility muses, "There is no danger …"

"Water is warm, coffee is hot,

air is clear …" Abundance marvels

"Friends are free to share this day …"

Creativity ponders

"Watch," Love prompts

as canvas continues to unfold

Person stands before mirror,

fingers moving through

tangled hair.

"Watch eyes meeting reflection"

Curiosity speaks first,

"Fear. Those eyes see fear"

"Fear of Person!!" adds Possibility

"The *Gap*," Presence realizes

Love nods, "This fear

is wrapped —

in clothes draped,

remembered,

held dear

and named *Trauma*. Its

special place

always near"

Curiosity dances

creating a path

Love continues,

"Part of the tangle,

Trauma fortifies *Gap.*"

"Ah, what clever way through! Person

creates a map," Creativity chimes,

"*Trauma* navigates movement

in *Gap*."

"I see! There is connection,"

Love exclaims,

"a path surely does form!"

Invention takes canvas from easel,

as each turns to their seat

Little Giants arrive

with water and treats

Strawberries and asparagus spears

meet marveling mouths

Sun brushes horizon

Twigs birth buds

Cormorants land treetops

Robins perch for new-day calling

As friends join morning walk,

"ohhing" and "aahing" bloom

where bloodroot and trillium

sparkle fresh dew

Taking path to fire's round,

Invention adds logs

Picking up canvas, Curiosity sees

Person driving car

on crowded avenue. Presence notices

fear pulsing,

radiating over pavement.

Puzzled, Possibility raises a wondering

brow, "Naturally, creation has invented

with ease

Yet, fear tangles

what's seen,

even as trust clearly weaves.

"Tho each has a place,

it's tangle that's known

and brought

where they meet,

even where most wish to move

gracefully on glorious feet."

Curiosity watches as Person

moves along day. Finally,

Person considers menu

for dinner to eat.

Curiosity takes deeper breath,

reaching for a hand to touch

Presence steps over and

embraces Curiosity who murmurs,

"I simply do not see a moment

for creativity's trace"

"And what of connection?"

"No, it seems that absence of one

easefully precludes the other"

After pause,

"In midst of such beauty,

Person sees no abundance – no love,

no reflection of self

"With so much unseen, ease is missed ...

innocence passed by,

but for a few – who

pause for special moments,

song or a sunset,

a puppy or painting

to carry the day"

Everyone turns as Love

she observes,

"This then is *Ache*."

In Possibility's hand, Innocence squirms,

"*Ache* radiates from these hearts!"

In bursts of excitement, wonder

circles all 'round

"What will it take?"

"For Love to thrive there?"

Whirls of light

emerge between tree roots

wafting gentle brilliance

across the horizon

"In each heart

Love lives

to be free..."

(The circle quiets)

"We've felt

fear

pulsing *Ache*

when

what simply Is

is not seen

not heard or believed," Love recalls

Creativity ponders, "What will it take?"

A loon calls from afar

"Sound?"

 Murmurs rise,

"Sound carries Love …"

"echoes all that is …"

"… all the weaving holds"

Growing boisterously still, Little Giants grin

Abundance and Innocence sit with Ease

as Presence and Invention

join Possibility and Curiosity

around the circle

with Creativity and Love

They sit in a pause

as trees flower pink,

daffodils nod and lilacs

meet in cozy conversation

with winged bumbles from bees

Sun inches higher

Forest grows greener

Baby bunnies leave their burrow

and bear cubs learn to climb

Our friends stir

and goslings squawk

It begins with a sniff,

scratch of a head

When they burst from seats

and jump giggling

to each other's arms,

Little Giants know

inspiration has sounded

Love goes to the river

placing hands in water's current

"Here," she nods,

"Love continuously flows"

Curiosity lifts and glides

as Creativity and Invention twirl

'round and 'round, filling

forest with airborne

delight

Possibility joins Ease, placing

newly found seeds in earth

promising, "Growth

will remember ..."

"freely given nourishment,"

Ease assures

Innocence wiggles wild ears

Presence and Abundance place palms

on bark-crevassed-trees,

joining rooted stability

that brushes clouds

welcoming all

to live free

Love murmurs with the river,

"We join with all

here in our weaving ... a weaving of all

Reverberating

an inviting sound"

As voices tone,

forest echoes

Snake and owl

Fawn and bat

Persons curling to nap

and waking for day,

all hear what Little Giants know ...

the sound of weaving

Sound realizing itself

as never before

Once Upon this Time

Elizabeth Jo experiences life as continuous conversation. As part of this conversation, she invites readers to curiously engage, immersing in exploration of themselves, each other, and our world. Her life is about shifting the kaleidoscope to open new possibilities.

We hope you'll join

conversation 'round the fire

www.choosingnewwaysforward.com

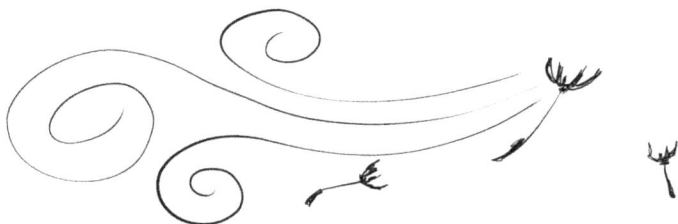

A small taste of Book 4, *Where We Meet*

(forthcoming 2025)

You are invited to a time
long anticipated

Amidst trees,
Humans
are gathering in a clearing
around a fire

Eight generations
are joining the circle,
young children
arrive with curious anticipation
for the very
first time

As this
Once Upon A Time
continues to unfold …

Person, full of complexity and a drive to know,

tumbles past window's edge ...

following Sound,

taking us

on a journey of discovery, walking with us

through growth and change —

in this story

that speaks to all parts of who we are

www.ingramcontent.com/pod-product-compliance
Lightning Source LLC
Chambersburg PA
CBHW050824090426
42738CB00021B/3477